UNHINGED SYLLABLE

SWASTIKA CHOWDHURY

Contents

1. An Unknown World — 1

2. We Grew Up — 2

3. If — 4

4. One More Time — 5

5. At Times — 6

6. Nobody — 7

7. A Sinner's Tale — 8

8. The Dark Fairy Tale — 10

9. Farewell — 12

10. Perfection — 14

11. Is A Lie.. — 17

12. A Letter To The End — 20

13. Self — 22

14. Song Of Fate — 24

15. This Mad Girl's Love Song — 28

16. To Kill To Die — 30

17. Things — 32

18. Timepiece — 33

19. Weight — 34

20. Song Of Void — 36

1. An Unknown World

I see the unknown,
clogging apart
from the chunks of riddles of life.
And yet it was far,
in the sphere of chimera and proclivity.
Where a twisted psyche meets something that satisfies its crave.
Still if tomorrow never comes,
I shall dwell behind the silhouette of the moon,
where the soul resides in solitude.
But now when I look into the dark,
I get a peek into another world.
A world beyond any conviction.
A world so flinty.
A world full of competence and enigma.
A world full of seclusion and gloom.
A world yet unknown.

2. We Grew Up

We grew up.
After all these years of lethal ache.
We grew up.
In the middle of the daylight hours,
when the wrecked miniatures
could bring tears,
until when we smile
with the rented hearts we bear.
We grew up.
When screeches were at most means
to intimate outrage in teens,
until the mankind believes
in saintly gestures and vicious afterthoughts.
We grew up.
From the day your love flooded my heart,
until now when its dry spelled
and not a single drop I have felt.
We grew up.
From the day I wanted to hold on,
until now when I want to beat a retreat
but my entity made me cheat.

The set is not set but a rise instead,
but my dawn became dusk

SWASTIKA CHOWDHURY

since my esse was dead.

3. If

If the world was black and white,
would the twilight recast into the light of the day?
If Apollo turned overcast,
won't I be reckoned?
If Selene didn't have blotches,
would mine ebb too?
If my known were unknown,
would I be able to shroud behind the silhouette of the righteous?
If I were you,
would I be received favourably?
If everything has an end,
why do these controversies doesn't have an epilogue?

At the hellmouth on the judgement day,
the saintly may slaughter the subconscious of the blest master,
but would the sinister be penalized too?

4. One More Time

One more time,
she was graced with pieces of bric-a-bracs.
One more time,
she was bartered for aurous.
One more time,
she payed homage to the stony broke.
One more time,
she was mislaid in mine shaft.
One more time,
she extricated nonpareils in the celestial city.
One more time,
she was deflowered by mates with ogre bosoms.
One more time,
the paragons of virtue have deceased.
One more time,
she was penalized for the fall from grace that didn't had her epithet.
One more time,
she became an enigma after the triumph over the barbarian.
One more time,
she became the phenomenal woman.

5. At Times

At times she is full of peril and mystique.
At times she lacks malice.
At times she is intimidated to be lifted by the unrevealed.
At times she hails the blizzard and fosters it.
At times she takes haven in contour.
At times she becomes their dynast of equity.
At times she is a modish sire.
At times she is a iniquitous vandal.
At times she carries out the wishes of the holy.
At times she puts her pennons and executes serenity.
At times she bows to the eternal.
At times she herself becomes the daemon.
At times she is the teeny lass.
At times she becomes the matriarch around the sphere.

6. Nobody

I am a nobody in this world.
Just a psyche held captive in a desolate chamber.
Just a duplet of mystified eyeballs ogling at the vault.
Just a pot of stale joe kept in the cloverleaf of a grubby desk.
Just those frozen drizzle of cloudburst on the window pane.
Just those penumbra in the faint light who stow away.

I am nobody in this world.
Just another light on the periphery of going out.
Just another entity whose time has run out.

7. A Sinner's Tale

I am a sinner,
biding in this sublunary cosmos.
I am an oodle,
of fallacies and pangs of conscience.
I am a mass,
of agony and fury.
As in to perceive my recital,
you need to bury yourself
in my memoir of hell.
For I am a sinner and this is my tale.
How I metamorphosed into dark.
How I nipped in the bud of my benevolence.

How I became disdainful.
How I endeavoured to run elbows with the ephemeral world.

And how I missed the boat.

How I used to cower before those behemoths into the murk.
And how I took them under my wing.
How I stayed put in the interim of dawn.
And how I lurk around during the hours of darkness.

How I attempted for the corporal vehemence.

And how I backed the wrong horse wretchedly.
How I triumphed and hit the bottom synchronously.

O my savant.
If you're still scrutinizing,
have the goodness to flee.
For the monstrosity,
from the briny
would come for you.
Enshroud my journal somewhere chasmic.
For my heart was sinful.
For the reason that
I am a sinner.

8. The Dark Fairy Tale

Out of the way where life crosses the great divide
Was the realm where the demons stride

Amidst the dusky and crooked critters
A revenant celibate was held as a prisoner
Hours and hours she wailed in pain
But all her tears went in vain

Then transpired a paedophile with paws of death
Trespassed her bosom and scared her fate

He sealed her lips to pause her screams
And slaughtered every part of her miniature dreams

This went on for over an year
Till the little Princess lost the utmost drizzle of fear

She mopped her tears and posed her crown
Assembled a conclusion of not letting herself down

She spent her days in ripping hearts
And her nights were destined for learning parts

She was the receptacle of duplex entity beneath her dress;

One the highbrow and another the agony benefactress.

She was allure enough to captivate anyone around;
She was also brutish enough to amplify their sobbing sound.

Seasons kept changing themselves, summers after autumns.
But she always had equilibrium of deep frost inside her atriums.

Until the Love came to her dark pavement;
To aegis her with great affection, most probably attachment.

But she wasn't able to grasp such warm intimacy,
She felt darkest aurae of anger, greif and anxiety.

The aurae were so brawny that they torned the girl in segments;
Those chunks still flow through our circulatory, as seven sin's cases.

9. Farewell

Adios to the grey and modish,
it's cynical to dwell.
All the probable hours of darkness,
murk engulfs me
and suckles on a lump of my soul.
How I crossed swords with incubus in my brainbox and berth.

Adios to the rest,
you have no knowledge about me.
How I found solace in solitude.
How I buried my soul behind absurdity.

Adios life,
you know a part of me.
The lump which was kicking her heels
for the final exit to secrete in his embrace.
How perfection became a lie.
How I introspected I could pull it through.
But I have diminished low.
We will run into each other someday mates, when the time is ripe and
fine.
But I cannot give the green light to my penumbra to influence people.
Remember me in tales and secrets.
Tell them I fought hard.

Adios to the grey and modish,
for my time has run out.
And I must pass.

10. Perfection

In the time of shadow and in radiance.

In solitude and amidst the crowd.

I perceive and endure it,
Pitching in like an opioid through my veins.
Amidst the crowd and in solitude.
I catch a sight of that jaws
Of that demon under my bed.
I can see it in the corner of my room.
Slurping in the shreds,

Of the illuminating euphoric pieces,

Deserting my entire system.
I attempt to recompense it with liquor.
I can see how it whirls, on its own melody,

Reciting a lone vocable.
"Perfection. Perfection. Perfection".
I struggled.

I struggled and yelled back.
"It's a lie. It's a lie. It's a lie."

I'm fatigued, petrified and parched.
My system is declining.
My muscles are stiff, bones don't hold.
But I can still hear the voices.

I question my fragile consciousness,
"Is this mine?" "Am I dead?"
Presumably, yes.
I'm a blackbird serving the leigh.
It echoes through the walls, this time. "Perfection. Perfection. Perfection."
I yell again.
"It's a lie. It's a lie. It's a lie."
Desertion aches my conscience.

The agony of being the forsaken
pierce its way through my bones.
I yell to put an end to the voices.
"I feel too."
Opium is pushed through my veins again.
My limbs go numb.
I collapse.
I overhear whispers, this time.
"Perfection. Perfection. Perfection."

I feel the orator's lips parting
Over my tired ears. "Perfection. Perfection. Perfection."

It slowly turns dark

As my lips quiver a bit, this time.
And a faint wail escapes in submission.
"It's .... Perfection."

11. Is A Lie..

"It's a new day. Just for you."
I bestir myself,
As the light of the day
came into contact with my pale skin.
The figures on the timepiece says
that it was just yesterday.
But my psyche claims that I was resurrected.
I hear it again.
"It's a new day. Just for you."
I feel feathery and transparent.
I feel the stream of dopamine
pushed through my veins.
I question my consciousness,
if I was hallucinating.
The burns and slits,
that rope hanging from the roof,
those emptied bottles, soiled dishes,
cigarette buds, said otherwise.
I questioned myself
if everything was a dream till now.
I questioned my borderline mind
if I was healed.

I hear it again.

"It's a new day. Just for you."
I shrug the questions off my shoulders.
I stepped towards the light of the day.
That sudden rush of dopamine
unblemished the blemishes of the mess.
I gazed all around me
at the spotless room,
the wrapped up files.

I catch a glance of something.
But that's not possible.
It was a dream.
"Every bit of it was a dream." I yelled.
I hear whispers
coming from the corner of the room.

That demon beneath my bed
is embracing me with open jaws.
It is engulfing every bit of me.
I'll be dispatched there again.
The place I dreamt.
The traumas I dreamt.
I yelled again.
"It's not true."
I scrutinized the ailing wounds and burns.
They were the pawns of the voices.
But it was all a dream.
I attempt to dispel my doubts.
I am being pulled

towards the blues,
being their black dog.

My lips quiver in submission, again.
My limbs go numb, again.
I collapse, again.
"It's a lie." I whisper.
"Is it?" Echoed the walls.

12. A Letter To The End

I am petrified yet so in love.
I am terrified of you,
even so you and me are of a piece.
For all one knows,
I am terrified of myself
or the mayhem you bring to being in me.
By all means,
you coerce my conviction.
You oblige me
to raise a dispute with my own actuality.
You resuscitate the blemishes
I ought to leave on the other side.
You rekindle the flavour of stale blood.
You provide me with brush of death
I have been yearning for.
For the reason that, you intimidate me.
You gaze at my unveiled subtle skin.
You spit truth.
You make me long for the life,
I was granted but never lived.
You demolish me
And you mould me afresh.
You bring the world to naught
only to mould it into being.

By all means, I fear you.
So does the world.
Even so for the world hereafter,
I have fallen into your arms.

For you are the ravager.
For you are the shaman.
For you are the storm.

13. Self

I close my eyes
and wake up to
an unfamiliar and strange world yet again
It was familiar to my eyes
when it was only dark foggy and opaque
It terrified my soul at first yet befriended it eventually
But as the nights went
it started forming shapes,
some took form of my fellow beings
and some of the dead,
some I not know as a part of the living.
With the time flying,
the shapes started throwing knives
at my undead body
Some of the wounds remembered it's sire
and some just whimpered in their forgetful manner.
Some were just young to bleed
and some just remained as dried scars.
It drained my soul of its energy drop by drop.
All it was left with
was the taste of stale blood, sweat, mucus, stained clothes.
A touch deprived body and an egoistic yet lonely soul
Only rage in mind
and the throbbing pain in the heart remained.

Only the screams with no voice
and the feeling of the fall were left as souvenirs.

And now when I stare
at the gateway of the two worlds,
mine looks different than my piece's.
I stare at it for it never lies.
I stare at the reality
and the reality stares back at me.

14. Song of Fate

What I seek was never contentment
like a cool breeze on a cloudless day of summer,
or like the initial sunbeam touching the face of one's bewitched soul
and leaves one wreathed in smiles.
But I have known for a while
that my fate would never grant me
the favour of atonement.
It was the perpetual shadow of uncanny lore
and the unceasing turmoil in the inside,
like I am running down the aisle of death
tailed by the same,
yet the escapade goes on, till the soul tends to depart.
Was I living?
I wasn't.
But I sure was alive.
"Did you tell them?"
I did as many times as your mind can presume.
I screamed at fate.
I screamed at the fate that resides in me.
The eerie yet preordained murk residing in my consciousness
that sits on a pile of bones laughs.
Its sardonic laughter deafens my ears
yet fails to petrify my soul.
But it scars my wounded psyche.

It makes the blue in my heart lose red,
red yet stale;
rotten but not dead.
It took the resemblance of the lake
that quenches the thirst of mortals.
Where once children came to heal
and escape from the demon under their bed.
Many sunsets and many sunrises later,
the mortals deserted it.
The lake bled too in its blue.
It bled for the solitude
because the living declared it guilty of honesty.
They abandoned their sire.
They lost faith on the bell of gospel,
the bell that swayed in the wind
that welcomes death.
as they stared deep down the abbys
and the abbys echoed
It echoed.
It echoed the pain.
"Did you tell them what you seek?"
I did,
as loud as a parade of soldiers with chest swelled with pride,
as they cheer and march down the streets of the homeland, they had to
take leave from.
I told them what I seek was peace.
What I seek was monotony.
What I seek was the tedious sameness
in landscape that exists

and lives all at one time.
That thrive life force from its repetition.
What I seek is the circular motion of the timepiece,
ticking everywhere
which makes the heart tremble yet thrilled?
What I seek was life in the monotonous world where the uncertainty
would
lie in the ageing of time and not in its ticking.
Where the sun might not be bright consistently.
Where even the dull days seem to exist
yet the existence of uncertainty
is not always correlated with agony.
Where gloom is beauty
and beauty is gloom
and none of it is bloody.
You see I do fear blood
But I want to bleed
as long as my consciousness abandons my body.
But my blood should only be red
my blood should not rot
My wounds should age well before I bleed again.
My heart should not be filled with blue and fear
as I drain it with liquor and smoke.
It should be machinated like any other.
My world should work like any others
My eyes should only see darkness when it sleeps and not wander around in
the worlds
where uncertainties turn themselves
into vicious monsters

and try to crack the glass of my existence.
My life should be fuelled and not dragged.
I should walk through the stairs
as I go up or down, I should not be
My skin should not be numb
and heart should not ache
every time the sun sets.
It should pour down from the heaven
and not my eyes.
The burns of my rage should get healed
before it gets ignited again.
My existence should make a meaning
and not misery.
You see what I seek was never lustre it was light.
What I seek was sanity not happiness.

15. This Mad Girl's Love Song

You awake my memories of a road in middle of nowhere,
embellished with decayed bones and blood,
that leads to the last resting place
of an unknown owner.

And how you sit in between my world and yours
like a deadly yet pale silhouette,
dressed in moonlight,
humming that can deafen any mortal,
licking blood off my bare wrists.

Or the euphoria deep inside
that comes with the haste motion
as I hear you fall,
or is it the rush
that comes from the red
that starts forming at the "lip of the slash",
or the ecstasy
of painting shades of your existence with mine
like a mad priest does for their sire.

Was it petrifying

when I closed my eyes
while you whispered my name
and how you twisted my life force into a knot in your fist,
to it was on the brink of
cracking the glass door
that separates us.
Instead it kindled the flame
to paint you the omen with the colour of my veins
that unleashes you
over the futile world.

And at times,
I desire
to cut my back open,
so the wings can sprout out
and fly my lifeless body away.
Or if my veins inside the mowed down chest
still flows the red.

or maybe
I should just
"shut my eyes and all the world drops dead.
(I think I made you up inside my head.)"

16. To Kill To Die

"You do not.
You do not shut your eyes.
Instead you get lost among the dead."

Yet sleep didn't embrace me once.
"Did you tell them you couldn't sleep?"
So even windows get barred?
So my thoughts
get clouded with pills of rainbow
that changes the colour of my veins?
I would rather munch through shards of glass,
as the redness drips from the edge of the curve,
and slip into the void to never return.
Than having arms unknown
restraining my lifeless body,
as I shut my eyes this time
not to wander about worlds beyond this
but to shaking with blue jolts.

I would wander amidst nowhere
with thoughts
that could pierce through my metal skin.

I would fall the big fall

yet not be an empty whole.

17. Things

All the things
that fly by night,
that seep through the skin
like worms on rotten flesh.
The things burrowed deep down
that bark less but bite more.
The borrowed things
that tear the flesh through their canines
like hungry hyenas feeding on a lion's flesh.
The things
that are carried,
that does not leave right away.
That are dug out with dirt
and the skin that gets ploughed.
The things
that was denied from rest
and found solace within unrest.

18. Timepiece

*My wrists are bare
dressed in scars
that paints the past
in red and violence.
The watch that ticks and tracks
the godless world and its liege,
now just sits there
without its ticking and tracking
calling for the harbinger
with fluttering wings,
dressed in night
that calls the unknown ruler
back from dead.
And I sit here
rocking the swing
to and from
this world and many others
sit on the hands
of an infinite timepiece
yet playing with its seconds.*

19. Weight

I can no longer bear
the weight of breath,
the weight of hunger,
the weight of thirst,
the weight of not being enough,
the weight of being too much,
the weight of love from all ends,
the weight of identity.
I yearn to be trapped
in a mason jar,
scratching on its walls
for mellow escapade,
with broken nails and dried blood.
To breathe in seconds
through cracks.
To gasp through a million existences in one
and finally, to leave an empty skeleton behind.
To have parasites brawl over the lifeless body of mine.
Its aches to ferret about for life
in every nook and cranny.
To die one time
and then resurrect the other.
To wipe the red off the floor and
to suck the one dripping through the skin,

to bridge over its lip cynically
as I go back to the jumbled heap from the state of rest.
I bide my time for the ones to exorcize
the sardonic laughter of the void in me
that reeks of decay
and cracks bones like sticks.
When I scream at the sky,
my words entangle and the letters vanish into the wind.
My voice goes unheard in the air,
like detangling one heartstring from another.
I can no longer bear
the weight of being alive.

20. Song of Void

My void speaks to me.
Oh, not the rustling of dry leaves in winter afternoons,
more like crickets rubbing their hands together at night.
My void speaks to me
And yearns for the end,
by weaving the urn of fate backwards,
pulling every string, every thread, back to unveil a discreet soul beneath
the empty skeleton.
My void speaks to me.
"Why are you absent?"
"Oh, is that the mark?"
"It's mating with your dead skin.
Paint it more red."
My void speaks to me.
"Did you not stop?
Did you not freeze?
The split second that rose "to get hit or to not" as the question.
And the flames that burst through the marrowless bones,
So cold that did not burn the hands restraining the ghostly tentacles you
drag around
My void speaks to me
So loud it deafens my ears
The voices burst through my eardrums to seek escape
My void speaks to me

I think it's a man with leather belt
that marks my skin, red, blue, purple
It fills my skull with a commonplace called grief, an illness to be solved
with more pills.
My void speaks to me.
It screams "I cannot sleep".